THE BOOK OF DESTRUCTIONS

Margarita Vélez Verbel

English translation by Maria Del Castillo Sucerquia

Edited by Douglas Cole

Unsolicited Press
Portland, Oregon
www.unsolicitedpress.com
info@unsolicitedpress.com
619–354–8005

THE BOOK OF DESTRUCTIONS
Copyright © 2026 Margarita Vélez Verbel
Copyright © 2026 Maria Del Castillo Sucerquia
All rights reserved in both Spanish and English.
Printed in the United States of America.
First Edition.
ISBN: 978-1-963115-89-5

This book is copyrighted material. The poems were first written in Spanish, then translated into English, and they belong entirely to the author and translator. That means: no photocopying, scanning, cutting, pasting, plagiarizing, pirating, remixing, or passing these words off as your own. Seriously—don't.

We know how tempting it is to share good poetry, but here's the deal: share the book, not the theft. Buy a copy for a friend, request it at your local library, or tattoo your favorite line across your chest if you're feeling extra committed. Just don't break the law or screw over the artist who put their blood, sweat, and words into this.

Published by Unsolicited Press, where we don't play by the industry's tired rules—but we will protect our authors' rights like hell.

Distributed by Asterism Books
https://asterismbooks.com/

For wholesale orders:
Asterism Books
568 1st Avenue South, Ste 120
Seattle, WA 98104
(206) 485-4829
info@asterismbooks.com

Cover Design: Kathryn Gerhardt
Editor: Douglas Cole

CONTENTS

PART I: *INSUBORDINATES*

    PRAISES TO SATAN   15
    MADAME BOVARY   16
    THE SHE-WOLF   17
    PRAISE TO THE CLITORIS   18

PART II *BELIEVERS*

    JOHN THE BAPTIST   21
    REDEMPTION   23
    DAD   24

PART III *FAMILY*

    ROOMS   26
    FAMILY HERITAGE   27
    THE SOUPS   28
    CHILDHOOD   29
    THE HOUSE   30
    NIGHT   31
    MATERNAL LOVE   32
    MOTHER   33
    ANOTHER CIGARETTE   34
    BRIEF BIOGRAPHICAL DATA OF THE AUTHOR   35
    I AM   37
    MEMORY   38
    YOU   39
    GO   40
    VERSE II   41

EACH MAN	42
SKETCH	43
ATTEMPTS	44
DESOLATION	45
THINGS	46
SLOWLY	47
BORN	48
EVERYTHING	49
OTHER LIVES	50
DREAMS	51
AT THE DEPTHS	52
THE HOUSE	53
VERSE	54
HOLLOWNESS	55
MEMORIES	56
MISENCOUNTER	57
WEARING MYSELF OUT	58
SEA	59
TRACES	60
WHIP	61
GLORY	62
SECONDS	63
INFINITE	64
DEEP	65
DEATH	66
ON FIRE	67
BEGINNING	68
ANIMAL	69
OLD AGE	70
FALLING	71
BEING	72
RAIN	73
WRITING	74

FLEETING	75
BODY	76
LIFE	77
CHIMERA	78
ATLAS	79

When a woman writes, she writes for all those who have stayed silent — for a thousand years, still silent — and will remain silent.

Marina Tsvietáieva

For Carmen Sofía Verbel Iriarte.

For Sara Duque, in memoriam.

For my childhood female friends and companions,
Diana Ricardo Garcia and Nubia Ballestas Merlano.

THE BOOK OF DESTRUCTIONS

Part I

Insubordinates

PRAISES TO SATAN

Wonderful angel,
god of the underworld,
redeemer of mankind,
who descended into the abyss and refused to be subdued.
Rebellious angel,
receive my body and my spirit.
Make me lustful,
give me a large, eager clitoris.
Give me passions.
Give me life.
Make me human, infinitely human.
For this, fill me with flaws,
great Satan, who indulges mankind.
Give me wine to numb me
when my spirit finds no joy
and let misfortune crumble me.
Great father of mine, I am born from your entrails,
noble warrior, Icarus, Prometheus,
light born of exile and humiliation,
redeemer of mankind,
of those who fight, of those who do not cower before power,
of those who question, of those who seek their freedom.
My angel.

MADAME BOVARY

You married so quickly, almost without knowing. One night, you were surrounded by guests, dressed in your wedding gown, and beside those carriages with people who treated you with solemnity and called you Mrs. Bovary.

They had your life all mapped out, your destiny chosen, while you read romantic novels and yearned for distant, exotic places. You carried other lives with you, other dreams, and Dr. Bovary was a good man, but he was no hero, no window into that world. So mundane, he could offer you nothing but mending his socks and sitting by the warmth of the hearth.

You were seduced by adventure, by the urge to set your imagination and body into a stampede, and you sought it in other men and places. How could they expect to keep you by the hearth, calmly waiting for one day to blend into the next?

You gave yourself over and over to each lover, though they would later leave, afraid of you, of your freedom—like all men are when a woman shows herself not as their maiden or servant, but as the mistress of her own self.

Yet still, you found your own happiness in surrender and in dreaming. When it all ended, when everything collapsed, you chose to leave in a sip of poison, where no husband, no family could touch you, chain you.

THE SHE-WOLF

The emperor's wife, Livia, the She-Wolf, as Claudius called her at the end of his days,
was the one who always remained by power, or behind it, or in some place where she could at least catch a glimpse of it. She claimed to have killed more men than Julius Caesar in battle, without ever carrying a sword.

An expert poisoner, she had always freed the palace from its fiercest enemies and protected the imperial family. She was more intelligent, more astute in wielding power than Julius Caesar and even Augustus, and had managed to keep Caligula in check, the only being on Earth she feared.

At the end of her days, the She-Wolf would ask herself: "Why doesn't Rome choose me as its emperor?" while muttering her tragedy for not having been born a man, so she could control that crowd of fools that was the imperial family, and thus directly rule the fate of Rome and the world once and for all.

PRAISE TO THE CLITORIS

My grand and beautiful clitoris, king of my vagina,
absolute owner of my delight.
Oh clitoris that grows on contact with my fingers,
little elf hidden among the petals of my vulva
who doesn't subordinate to anything,
who is enough for herself,
who hides in my hands as a bird,
Clitoris, a place only mine where no one can reach me.
A place of liberty for my body and my spirit.

Part II

Believers

JOHN THE BAPTIST

He was not worthy to unstrap the sandal of the one who would come after him, said John the Baptist, as he lashed out at Salome's mother through every street of his province. "Whore," he would shout to the crowds every time the woman crossed the public squares, for she had slept with some little soldier of her husband, a general of five suns.

"Whore," he would shout whenever he could, jubilant, exalted, like a madman, in a kind of mystical ecstasy. He was the same John who recited the Old Testament, the Psalms of King Solomon, who had bedded around two thousand women, most of them young girls, barely eighteen years old, who were forcibly taken by their fathers as prizes for a man anointed by God—the wise one who claimed them, then took them from his bed as if wiping himself with a napkin—small girls trembling in fear at the imminent pain of surrendering to a man who had succumbed to the passage of time, filled with scars and ugliness.

Nothing ignoble did John see in the great sage, nor in Abraham, who ate and impregnated just like Hagar in the same tent. For them, as for the rest of the prophet rapists and abusers of women and girls, he never went out screaming in the streets of Jericho. Nor did he receive any message from his most high god to indicate there was any affront, any blemish in these high chosen ones that offended him. But before that woman, it was different: she was a whore because she enjoyed her body abundantly, reveled in her female vigor, and became ecstatic with one soldier or another of her husband, occasionally caught in the standing position. John, the disgraced one, the one who saw the speck in the eye of others but not the beam in the eye of Judaism.

There was never a head more justly cut off.

REDEMPTION

Christ admonished those who threw stones at the adulterous woman, telling them it was wrong, for we are all sinners, and no one could cast the first stone. But his brief judgment failed to question that stoning a woman was inherently vile, immoral, and inhuman, regardless of whether her executioners were saints or sinners.

Christ told them to give to God what is God's, and to Caesar what is Caesar's, but he never questioned why there were so many things for Caesar and for God, and so few things for everyone else.

Paul, the apostle who spread Christianity, said that women should obey their husbands as slaves obey their masters. He taught the poor to remain in poverty, to see it as a sign of blessedness, and taught children to submit to their parents. This Christianity, said Paul—the misogynist, the one who fought against all philosophy, all forms of rationality and science, against any possibility of freedom—would grant us redemption.

Christianity and its absurdities taught men to obey: slaves to their masters, women to their husbands, children to their parents. Christianity stripped human beings of the most sacred thing they had: their freedom, their innate rebellion, their ability to change what oppresses and degrades them.

DAD

Judeo-Christian, you understood your Catholicism
and your conservative party,
and through your Laureano Gómez, you learned all the filth of
    power's misuse.
Despotic and violent, you treated your children and wife
like a storm treats debris.
Like a hurricane, you raged over the lives
of the fragile souls around you,
until you destroyed them from their very roots.

Part III

Family

ROOMS

What room is there for the sorrowful,
for the weary,
for the one who does not sleep in this house?
What room is there in this house for a bleeding heart?

FAMILY HERITAGE

For Carmen Sofía Verbel Iriarte
In memory of Sara Duque Bonolli

How much I suffer for my mother and grandmothers.
How much I suffer for their worlds reduced to stove and
      delivery rooms;
their debased lives, their slavery.
Poor little beings, poor butterflies of crying.
How much violence weighs them down,
how much violence lurks in their rooms,
in their skirts, in their copulation whose pleasure is exclusive
      to men.
How much silence hangs over their procreated children
born against their will,
like a agonizing iron spear stuck in the bellies.
How much shit hidden under the roof,
among hot lard and morning coffees.
How much rottenness.

THE SOUPS

I remember my mother well, with her crucifix made of seeds,
her rosary in hand.
I remember her repeating her Hail Marys
and explaining to her children the blessings of the kingdom
that her Jewish God would bring us.
I remember the mark of a blow on her eye, dealt by her husband,
telling us that God was just.
I remember her Christian resignation, her Carreño manners,
and Father Astete's booklet while she made soups.
I remember her scrutinizing eyes, probing the depths of my soul,
to prevent me from judging,
from questioning, from fighting,
from thinking, from seeing the shit up to my neck that the family
 was soaked in,
the indignity that reigned within those four walls.
I remember her Christian morality, her dog morality.
I remember her shoving her fucking Christianity into my eyes,
just like she did with the soups.

CHILDHOOD

For my sisters, Sara y Fanny

What loneliness was childhood,
what a dark time.
My dispossessed and blue body,
my wounded body.
What loneliness was childhood,
knowing myself helpless
in the mother's hands and father's whip.
What loneliness was childhood.

THE HOUSE

Four walls,
and the adults gravitating to that space.
We were small, caught between large and violent hands.
Four walls and captivity,
the fear of knowing we were alone, with nowhere to go.

NIGHT

I did not like the night.
My father arrived drunk, and I slept
sheltered in fear every night.
No one came at night to help me.
As with stalking wolves and dark forests,
the night always brought terror.

MATERNAL LOVE

Who gave you the right to bring me into this world?
Who gave you the right to bind me to you for life,
to carry me in your womb
for nine months, in communion with your navel?
Who gave you the right to place your hopes in me,
to put the weight of your old age on my shoulders,
expecting me to help when you grow old?
Who gave you the right to try to make me your extension,
to fill your emptiness, to carry
the frustrations your life leaves behind,
to quietly endure your anger as if I don't feel it,
to make me bear the weight of all the pain and injustice
       you've suffered,
just like every parent does to their child,
who, over time, announces their end: the new bone,
       the new marrow,
the new breath of life already fading in their flesh,
the dreams long gone, and in the end, their own death.
Who told you that I'm like a safe,
like a piggy bank, where you've deposited years,
dreams, things, expecting me to return them to you doubled?

MOTHER

My mother had no body
nor freedom; she had nothing—
only cigarettes she smoked compulsively,
which destroyed her throat.
In the midst of violence,
she suffered within those four walls,
with only a rosary and Christian resignation for company.
My mother had neither body nor soul.
My father stripped her of everything with his blows,
constantly humiliating her.
My mother died after giving birth to us:
laughter and life left her,
and only a shell remained,
where no blood or life flows.
I grew up with her like a weed in a graveyard.

ANOTHER CIGARETTE

Mother is old now, almost stiff.
I always remember her smoking one cigarette after another,
a grimace on her face, trapped in constant anxiety.
The smoke rising from her lungs
as a sign of surrender.
Mother working among her dirty dishes and foam,
shattering her throat with a hoarse, furious
defiance of life.

BRIEF BIOGRAPHICAL DATA OF THE AUTHOR

I write this poem so I don't forget that I am Margarita Vélez,
daughter of Pedro Vélez Duque and Carmen Sofía Verbel Iriarte.
That my childhood took place in Sincelejo.
That my father always came home drunk and beat my
      mother relentlessly.
That I lived these sad days with my siblings, Sara, Pedro,
      and Fanny.
That as a child, I went to school after not having slept all night,
assaulted by the fear of my father's sudden return
and the chaos that would follow.
I write this poem so I don't forget running desperately,
seeking help, knocking on my neighbors' doors,
filled with dread and the cold of the night.
That I slept with my clothes on, ready to flee.
That the next morning I attended algebra and biology class,
and stayed in the bathroom crying during recess.
That my mother thought I was distracted and stupid,
with sadness always close to the surface, tears constantly falling.
I know she worried about her daughter, the one who always
      lost things,
the strange one, the scatterbrained one.
I write this poem so I don't forget anything,
like how my rich cousins, the Moras,
gave me their old dresses,
and that's how I had clothes to wear.
So I don't forget that I went to school in tight shoes

from the year before, walking
through the mud and puddles in the humble neighborhood
    where I lived: La Lucha.
That while all of this was happening, literature got into my veins,
and I read voraciously, dreaming of becoming a writer.
I write this poem so I don't have to run out in the middle
    of the night
to ask my neighbors for help, always deaf,
always with their doors shut,
so that my mom knows I wasn't distracted, that I wasn't stupid.
I write this poem to tell everyone who was around me,
who saw me suffer, those who stayed silent, that I was
    never distracted,
that I knew everything and that this truth weighed on me,
and sank me like a stone.
I want to tell them that I was alert and vigilant,
like a condor over the plains.
I want to tell them that I opposed all of you
    and your indifference,
toward my father's violence, toward his machismo,
toward my mother's submission, with the strength and courage,
the dignity and decency that childhood gives us.
I write this poem to tell them that I was aware.

I AM

Who will have the same joy that I have now,
the same rapture of my spirit,
the same boldness in my eyes,
the same tranquility?
Who will have what I am now,
this contemplation of the meadow?
Who will have Margarita,
the part of me that lives now?
Who can decipher Margarita, the one who writes now
in a rapture of love
or hope,
the one who swallows herself in this very moment?
Who will know of Margarita, the one who lives in this line,
in her eyes, in her longing?

MEMORY

The days return.
Memory, like a carousel, always brings us
pieces of recollection.
There is a single howl within me today,
both the starting point and the destination:
humiliation and violence.
There is a house with its walls,
with its silences and fears, clinging to me
like my own bones.
Distant yet ever-present voices:
a beaten mother who reminds me
that, at least, revenge could redeem us.

YOU

Who will pay for all that you have done to me?
For all that you have taken from me.
Who among you, who knew me and left me alone,
who saw me suffer and passed by without a glance?
Who among you will pay for such infamy?

GO

To some day,
to some place that isn't here.
To somewhere none of this misery exists,
all the sterility that engulfs their lives,
their daily reality of hunger and death.

VERSE II

I write this verse
that I've already felt and now I shape.
I just want to know what mark it leaves behind.
I wish it would at least burn,
that it would make blood flow.
I wish it were a slap on someone's face.
I want this verse like a burst of gunpowder,
to make their souls jump.

EACH MAN

Each man walks this path of shadows,
figures that fade as he seeks what he desires.
Everything that is born dies
while he grows older, waiting,
all his goodness, all his drive, fading away.

SKETCH

There's barely enough time to remember, to understand, to sense each desire, each longing, as if we were in an eternal childhood. The life of each being is a miniature, a little one who barely murmurs, a poorly drawn sketch. Our life drifts further and further from our attempts.

ATTEMPTS

I begin to write, but I don't write.
I begin to die, but I don't die…
to beat, but I don't beat.
Difficult to write, difficult to die.

DESOLATION

A man can sit
and see all the sorrow around him.
He can understand how sad life is,
how pointless it seems.
The precariousness, the lowliness in every act.
The competition and the inhumanity he must embrace to survive.
For every loaf of bread he eats, ten men die without it across
          the street.
He knows that every man who lives is a predator of his own kind.
He knows that it's all hunger and desolation.

THINGS

Some things will remain still,
some things already dead in my hands.
There will be weariness and nostalgia,
memories like quiet pools,
some drops between the wet leaves.
Other things will remain as signs:
small footsteps in time.

SLOWLY

I move slowly on the paper,
sometimes revealing myself,
placing my finger on the wound.
I move blindly on the paper, discovering myself,
like a cocoon opening to the sun.

BORN

I am being born and dying
in this very moment,
like roses and grass,
like the calla lily and the tiger.
I am vast in this crackling,
in this storm of sensations,
in this pain and joy,
in this anguish and body that are part of the cosmos,
in my arms like branches of towering trees
and like the endless deserts.
In my mouth of cave and water
I am being born and dying in this very moment,
in a hard way,
with the urgency of a lathe,
with the fiery intensity of a volcano.

EVERYTHING

I won't live through it all.
I won't feel it all.
I'll be only a second, an instant,
fear, fleeting.
I won't be the Universe, nor the leaf.
I am an attempt, the grass.
The bird that soars through space.
That's why everything must be forgiven,
because I walk blindly against time.
Because I've fought despite losing,
despite suffering,
despite knowing I won't reach anywhere.

OTHER LIVES

Why does it sometimes feel like we're
living the lives of others,
as if their burdens, their souls
dwell upon our weary bodies?
Why were we given a time that wasn't ours?
One day, a useless hope, amid so much desolation and misery?
Why does it seem we are destined
to carry all the sadness, all the fatigue
of the world like a heavy barrel?

DREAMS

All we have left
is to believe in a loaf of bread,
in a different place
to keep from dying all at once.
All we can do is wait patiently
and think of a better day,
of a more fertile ground.

AT THE DEPTHS

There is no deeper sadness
than the one we feel,
nor a joy more intense than our own.
There is nothing, nothing outside
of ourselves.
There is no mirror to reflect the spirit,
nor its torments nor its melancholies.
There is nothing that dies with us and resurrects.
When we fall into the depths or rise to the peaks,
we are alone, terribly alone, pouring out our anguishes,
like lacerating substances,
corroded.

THE HOUSE

To arrive at any place
where it feels like time doesn't pass.
To arrive at any place where nothing exists,
where everything is lost.
To arrive at this place depopulated of the soul
without knowing or understanding why this anguish,
why this emptiness that cannot be filled,
that feeling of waiting,
that inner search that never calms.

VERSE

Neither verse nor pen knows
what the heart holds,
nor the impassive time,
nor sluggish memory clutching pieces of the past.
No one knows what I feel now:
this slow agony, this indecipherable anguish.

HOLLOWNESS

What is the feeling I have now?
What is this deep complaint that tears me apart?
I feel this hollowness,
this distant and deafening hum,
uncertain and murky.
What is this that attacks like a caged beast?
What is the day, what is the pain that resurrects today
from my flesh like an old enemy that reappears,
like an old infection,
like a wound poorly healed?

MEMORIES

Sensations do not come back,
time does not come back,
I do not come back.
What happens, what passes over us
is a memory, then the past.

MISENCOUNTER

I've gone out to fight for a loaf of bread,
to battle, to compete.
I've gone out as what I am: a lion, a vulture.
I've gone out with strength to bear this oppressive world.
I've gone out with my hunger and my bones
to wait, to fight, to debase myself.

WEARING MYSELF OUT

I must wear myself out. I must die.
I must do so many things.
I must press on with determination,
like crossing a row of thorns.
I must do it without complaining, hoping for I don't know what,
dreaming of I don't know what.

SEA

I am turned inward, like into a sea.
Sometimes calm, sometimes impetuous, sometimes hard.
I want peace, but it blinds me, covers me, drags me
to different, uncertain places.
I feel soft and watching, waiting.
Barely, sometimes, I know myself, and I fall silent in wonder
when from within me emerges, each new thing, each
        unsuspected passion.
I burn and shudder before myself
as before the strangest of beings.

TRACES

Will time leave us anything?
Will life leave us anything?
A little joy,
a little illusion,
a little room of innocence
after having fought and humiliated ourselves?

WHIP

I am in my time, which is my whip,
a harsh and authoritative master
that takes away my seconds and even my breath.
But why complain, if even the condor suffers it
and the beautiful orchid, without uttering a single sigh,
without lamenting.

GLORY

We live searching for a minute of glory,
a minute of peace after long and stormy days,
after a life-and-death struggle,
we want a rest.
We live for a day that never comes,
for a future joy,
like a dog chasing a bone.
And in the end, peace comes to us,
but not the peace of dreams fulfilled
but the peace of a battle lost.
Resignation comes to us, full of weariness,
like the solitude of a street on a Sunday afternoon.

SECONDS

I have a life that I burn up in seconds,
a body that ages a short time.
I have unease and anguish, uncontrollable desires.
I have a short time, like that of a caterpillar,
like that of a leaf falling from a withered tree.

INFINITE

This feeling will pass, any longing that overwhelms me will pass.
This day and this life of mine will pass,
like that of the tiny ant.
Every color will pass, like the simplest thing,
as if I were just passing through
each useless life, each sensation, each death,
each thing that is born and perishes, so insignificant
to the cosmos, like a speck of dust.
There is so much cruelty in the infinite,
in the absolute and inexorable arc of time.

DEEP

I gather this feeling now.
I gather now a part of me: warm, deep.
And I rejoice in my confusion,
in my discovery,
in my depth.

DEATH

When I finish writing this verse,
it will be past.
When this feeling passes,
another one will overcome me.
When I die
I will stop hesitating,
I will reach the pure thing,
the nothingness, the void,
immortality;
the eternal not being.

ON FIRE

In every moment we are different.
In every second, wrapped in a different passion.
So true, so suffering,
unable to distance ourselves from our own flame.
On fire.

BEGINNING

I begin within myself.
I fall like a drop of water.
I exhaust myself in this "me," in this time.
I wear myself out from within.
Pain, anguish, desires, movements.
Sweet, sour,
I fall, I enter, I live.
Everything in disorder, everything in motion.
I, immense, devour.
Seconds upon seconds galloping.
Emotions like colors,
like days falling over my body.

ANIMAL

What a terrible being I must have been for many.
How many have I taken bread from in this struggle to survive?
How many have I denied the space I occupy when I walk down
    the street?
How many have I not loved, as they drag a miserable life?
How many flowers do I crush as I walk?
And I've done it all with the greatest innocence,
like a cornered animal: hungry and scared.

OLD AGE

Soon I will have aged,
and I will dedicate myself to remembering,
to feeling nostalgia, to feeling alone.
Soon I will no longer be who I am,
just a city in ruins.
Every sensation will feel distant.
Every dream will be absent.
Soon I will have aged,
and I will wonder how I spent my time,
what has been enough for so little.
Who stole everything and left me discarded,
like a useless object.
What woman did I stop being,
what place didn't I know, what things
could I have done and didn't?
I will be hollow and late, longing for my young body
like a fresh river.
I will be the woman who ends all battles
against her eternal enemy: time.

FALLING

It seems like everything was falling inside of me,
everything in disorder,
everything inside my open chest: fear, anguish,
all the memories.
It seems like everything came all at once
and took me by surprise,
without me being able to resist.

BEING

I want to calm myself, fall,
be inside,
where nothing touches me.
Where this noise and the people boiling
in the streets with all their misery
that overwhelms me,
that shakes me,
doesn't touch me.
I want them to float away, not disturb me.
I want to calm myself, fall,
be inside.

RAIN

Some words rain down on the paper,
some sensations I don't learn,
some ideas I don't finish.
The words come and go, a little suffocated,
somewhat exhausted, battered.
The words come and go,
spinning like a carousel,
as if controlled by a puppeteer,
they come and go, imprecise.

WRITING

I begin to write this morning
in which I feel sadness,
a full and gentle sensation,
as if something is slipping away from my body.
I begin to write this verse
warm and fresh,
a line that cuts through this morning like a boat,
and I don't feel the need to shout.
I just remain immersed in the drowsiness and slowness
of my body, which today is a heron, like the damp grass,
like a cloud playing,
changing shapes.

FLEETING

What I write is fleeting,
a bird nesting in one winter season.
What I write drips from me drop by drop,
it is squeezed out like my blood,
it nests in my guts.
What I write is a mirage of my emotions,
a painful briefness like my being.
Anguish in search of the eternal.
Uselessness and unease.

BODY

I arrive at my uninhabited and sad body,
abandoned like a useless thing.
I arrive at myself, not to stay, but to flee.
I arrive at myself to hurt,
to sink into every part.
Dream and death of being.
Terrifying anguish.

LIFE

We live one life,
like a single stroke,
like a single course,
like an evening that dies
too early under the sun.

CHIMERA

A sunny day will come after,
and an eternal after will run through our veins.
An increasingly distant oasis,
a painful chimera.

ATLAS

Who hasn't been a prisoner of despair
and a victim of some wrong?
Who hasn't harbored resentment
and seen some hope die?
Who hasn't been painfully battered,
deprived down to the bones?
Who hasn't waited a long time for revenge
or to explode from some sharp, dull pain that devours them?
Who hasn't descended, only to find themselves
immensely alone before the world, like Atlas

ABOUT THE AUTHOR

Margarita Vélez Verbel, Corozal (Sucre) es autora de los poemarios:"Los ángeles sólo bajan una vez", "Espinas y cenizas", "Del polvo y el olvido", entre otros. Voz trágica y transgresora, la de Margarita se constituye en una de las más originales en el concierto de voces de mujeres poetas del Caribe

ABOUT THE TRANSLATOR

María Del Castillo Sucerquia , born in Barranquilla, Colombia (1997), is a bilingual poet, writer, literary agent, tutor, and translator. She has participated in numerous poetry festivals around the world and her poems have been translated into several languages and published in anthologies and magazines. She is a translator and columnist for the magazines Vive Afro (Colombia), Raíz Invertida (Colombia), Cronopio (Colombia), El Golem (Mexico), Palabrerías (Mexico), Poesía UC (Venezuela), Mood Magazine (Mexico), Atunys Poetry (Belgium), among others.

ABOUT THE EDITOR

Douglas Cole has published two novels and eight poetry collections. His first novel, *The White Field*, won the American Fiction Award. His poetry collection, *The Cabin at the End of the World*, won a Best Book Award for urban poetry and the International Impact Award. He writes the column, "Trading Fours," for the online journal *Jerry Jazz Musician*, including recorded collaborations with musicians. He has been nominated Eight times for a Pushcart and Nine times for Best of the Net. His website is https://douglastcole.com.

ABOUT THE PRESS

Unsolicited Press is based out of Portland, Oregon and focuses on the works of the unsung and underrepresented. As a womxn-owned, all-volunteer small publisher that doesn't worry about profits as much as championing exceptional literature, we have the privilege of partnering with authors skirting the fringes of the lit world. We've worked with emerging and award-winning authors such as Amy Shimshon-Santo, Brook Bhagat, Elisa Carlsen, Tara Stillions Whitehead, and Anne Leigh Parrish.

Learn more at unsolicitedpress.com. Find us on Instagram, X, Facebook, Pinterest, Bsky, Threads, YouTube, and LinkedIn. Unsolicited Press also writes a snarky newsletter on Substack.

www.ingramcontent.com/pod-product-compliance
Lightning Source LLC
LaVergne TN
LVHW090036080526
838202LV00046B/3846